How Normal People Create Their Wealth ... and you can too!

Wealth Workout™

The Simple Seven Step Formula for Financial Success

Hi Susannah

Marcus de Maria

Wealth Workout™ First published in 2009 by;

Ecademy Press

6, Woodland Rise, Penryn, Cornwall, UK. TR10 8QD

info@ecademy-press.com

www.ecademy-press.com

Printed and Bound by; Lightning Source in the UK and USA

Set in Myriad 11pt on 19pt by Charlotte Mouncey

Printed on acid-free paper from managed forests. This book is printed on demand, so no copies will be remaindered or pulped.

ISBN 978-1-905823-50-5

A CIP catalogue record for this book is available from the British Library.

Contents

Firstly, my thanks go to my wife and soul mate Mudrika, for her belief in me and unconditional support and love. I love you more and more each day.

To Mindy Gibbins-Klein who started me off and convinced me that writing a book really IS the right thing to do.

To my loving parents who are always there for me.

To my big brother Steve who continues to inspire me.

My father-in-law whose story of success reminds me of what is possible and that there is always a way.

To everyone who was involved and helped with the book.

To all my family of clients who have given me the privilege of working with them and sharing my knowledge.

And finally, to my daughter, Melania Shanta de Maria, whom I can't wait to meet in 3 months time.

A special note for you from the author

Congratulations on ordering your book. That is an awesome first step. The second step is to actually read it - did you know that on average only 10% of books get read? Or maybe you are better than average - ok then, let's prove it. Somewhere in the book, I have added a sentence which is totally out of context. If you find this sentence, you can claim your prize which we will send to you free of charge. But of course you will have to read the book first to find it. Good luck!

I know that reading this book AND taking action on its contents will totally change your life ... and the life of your family.

So here's my first challenge for you. Send me an email before you read the book at book@investment-mastery.com and tell me what you are hoping to achieve.

Here are 3 questions for you to answer when you email me:

- *What are your financial goals / aspirations?*
- *Why do you want to reach those goals?*
- *Why are you sick and tired of not having enough money to live the life of your dreams?*

Would you like one of our team to call you to explain how best to answer these questions or how we can help you? If the answer is yes, then please add your telephone number.

To your good Wealth!

Marcus de Maria book@investment-mastery.com

The best way to help the poor is not to become one of them.

Laig Hancock

Allow me to introduce myself: my name is Marcus de Maria, I am 39 years old and live in Kent with my lovely wife, Mudrika. I am a Stock market investor, author, trainer, and wealth mentor. I created my wealth through investing in other people's start up businesses; my wife invested in property and land and I specialised in stock market, Foreign Exchange and oil trading.

We are now financially independent, which means that we don't have to work for a living but can rely on our investments if we wanted to. We now mentor people who are serious about becoming financially wealthy.

But that wasn't always the case. When I started my wealth creation journey at the age of 29, I still hadn't had a job and knew nothing about wealth creation ... I had been studying and taking years off before university, during university, after university and then took on the longest postgraduate degree I could find - three years - and after that I took a year off. Anyway, I remember one evening having a discussion with my father.

My father started work when he was 17. To cut a long story short he had worked for the same bank all his life and I guess wanted something similar for my brother and myself. I had an offer on the table to join an international management consulting company. My father of course was adamant that this was the best step for me but I wanted to be an entrepreneur and work for myself. I told him this and he said, "You don't have any experience, what are you going to be an entrepreneur in?" So I replied, "I don't know, anything ... for example I will open a hot-dog stand (I still think they are very lucrative) and then have another and another and have a chain of them around the country."

How impressed do you think my banker father was with my hot dog stand idea?

Not very.

Anyway, after a prolonged testing of wills I gave in, thinking he must know something I don't. I worked for that company for three years and the last year was so depressingly bad that I actually ended up in hospital with stress related stomach pains. I had these attacks about every four weeks, I used to joke that they were like having a period but the pain was sometimes so bad that it was like giving birth – I was hyperventilating to alleviate the pain to such an extent that I was almost passing out and if there was anyone holding my hand I would crush it without realising what I was doing.

This was my body telling me in no uncertain terms that I was not meant to be in this job. Of course in hindsight it is easy to say, "then just leave" but when you are so close to something, you can't see the wood for the trees. The problem in my mind (and that is exactly where the problem lay) was that I was being paid well, I was scared of the unknown and, despite the pain, was sort of comfortable being where I was. The devil you know and all that.

Good pay, hate the job. What to do?

In the days when I was still reading newspapers I picked up a copy of The Evening Standard. In it was an advertisement for a life changing seminar called UPW - Unleash the Power Within – by Anthony Robbins. It seemed exactly what I was looking for but I was also cynical. The sales rep asked me two questions I will never forget. He said:

"What will happen if you carry on doing what you are doing now?" I thought about living a life without purpose or passion and shuddered. This was not an option.

Then he said, *"and what could happen if you come on to*

the seminar and change your life?" I instantly realised that he was right and signed up there and then. I went to UPW Cardiff in 1999 and he is right, life really was 'never the same again'.

When these rare moments come along, grab them with both hands.

Why does it take someone else to tell us that we are in total control of our own lives and destinies? I am not sure but sometimes we need someone to take away the uncertainty. By the end of the Sunday I left a message for my boss to meet with him first thing Tuesday morning. When I put down the phone I thought, "Shit, what have I done?" but to cut a long story short I fired my boss that Tuesday morning and I can tell you that it was one of the best and most liberating things I have ever done. I took control back of my own life.

But leaving a job means you need to make money, so I travelled to Germany to start a dotcom and lived for eight months without pay on someone's sofa. In the end, we managed to negotiate DM3.4 million (£1.15 million) for 10% of our company but the timing could not have been worse. We opened up the newspapers to find that the dotcom bubble had well and truly burst and we could not get hold of our benefactors for love nor money. This was disappointing because we had been so close and in the end I had to come back to the UK. I didn't want to work for anyone else so I took an internal consultant role with a company that had been voted the most innovative company in the ENTIRE world by Fortune magazine .. not once, or two years in a row, but seven years in a row. Everyone thought they were working for the most incredible company in the world. The name of the company?

Enron!

They were certainly innovative, that's for sure ... with their accounts. For those who don't know, they managed to hide $500,000,000 worth of losses whilst pretending to be hugely profitable. Their stock price, once in the $90s fell to zero and we all lost our stock options. It was the biggest accountancy scandal of its time and brought Arthur Andersen, the prestigious accounting company, to its knees and started a host of investigations that shook the business and accountancy world.

So this is all very interesting but it doesn't help my finances. I mean, reading this, you would probably agree that you like to have a roof over your head and you like to eat food, drink and go out now and again etc. Well, all I had was plenty of debt because don't forget I had been studying up until the age of 29 without any income and things were going from bad to worse. So I did what any normal person would do ... no, not get a job ... start a networking marketing company!

My brother and I spent 2 years really working the business, built up a good team in UK and abroad, were being promoted and honoured on stage but there was one teensy weensy little problem ... we weren't making any money. And as soon as we made some we were constantly encouraged to spend it all again by flying to international conventions with the team to motivate them. I personally know many people who have made a lot of money in a variety of these companies, in fact some of them probably wouldn't have managed to make money in other professions. One thing is for sure though: network marketing, multi-level marketing or referral marketing is a 3-5 year game plan, don't let anyone tell you any different.

I didn't have 3-5 years, I needed the money now. By this time I was £50,000 in debt and sleeping on my brother's floor in a bright green sleeping bag. You might be thinking, "Marcus, I've got a mortgage bigger than that", but I didn't even have that. This £50,000 was bad debt with nothing to show for it and no assets to my name.

I needed money right now. What would you have done?

Get a ...

That's right, I decided on another start-up business. This time a friend of mine approached me about a really amazing opportunity – invest in his start up company. The company had a neat invention to do with men's urinals. I figured that men have to pee so there had to be a market there.

When you need money for a start up you turn to the 3 Fs. Do you know what they are? Friends, Family and ... Fools. Well I think I was his Friend but anyway remember I didn't have any money so I had to turn around to my Friends, my Family and my Fools. They must have believed in me because I managed to raise around £100,000 to invest in this company.

So now I was seriously in debt so this thing had to work and for the next year or so I was working virtually for nothing making sure that my money and that of my people was going to be safe by helping the company with sales, something I hadn't really done before ... and it showed. We didn't make many sales, but we did get our product into key flagship locations, which turned out to be very important indeed.

To cut a long and excruciating story short, the CEO ran away with my £100,000 and I was left high and dry without share certificates, the original £50,000 in bad debt and now another £100,000 on top, which was owed to friends and family. Luckily I had forged a great relationship with the inventor of the product and we set about forming another company, replacing the shares, attracting venture capital and doing things the right way. The company was sold for just under £10 million to a big international washroom company a few years later so it all turned out ok.

Let's fast forward several years. We now own land and property in over five different countries, trade on the forex with millions on a daily basis, run several businesses and have invested in several start-ups.

What I wanted to share with you is my learning along the way ... and I had plenty of them. While I was building up my wealth I spent every spare second getting a financial wealth education second to none so that I could apply what I had learned in real life. And the results are truly amazing.

I want to share what I have learned with you right now, so let's get to it.

In my opinion there are 8 steps to wealth, each as important as the next. Take a look at the following:

1. Discover what is holding us back and deal with it
2. Find our financial vision and purpose
3. Plan for wealth
4. Understand what money is and attract it into our lives.
5. Understand financial concepts and the skills to create money
6. Create the support team we need
7. Take massive consistent wealth action
8. Reap the rewards and give back

Now what you might notice is that most of the points above have to do with mindset and not the skills. While the skills of making money are essential they only make up approximately 20% of the picture, and 80% of financial success is without doubt the mindset and psychology.

We are going to be dealing with steps one through seven in this book, so let's go through each of the steps.

Life's battles don't always go to the stronger or faster man. But sooner or later the man who wins, is the man who thinks he can.

Vince Lombardi

1: Discover what is holding us back

Think about this for a moment – whatever your financial situation, why aren't you further along? There are teenagers who have generated millions of pounds ... why not you?

I want to use a metaphor – imagine yourself as a tree, with your roots firmly in the ground. The fruits hanging from your branches are quite literally the fruits of your ... labour. The cars, houses, boats, etc. are the physical results of your actions. And your actions are the results of your thoughts. So thoughts are incredibly powerful things and there is one aspect I want to deal with and that is your beliefs about things. Most people don't know what their beliefs are. Why? Because just like the roots of the tree, they are hidden deep in the ground. but they are also what need the most nourishment. The tree cannot survive unless the roots get nourishment and water. And we are exactly the same.

Do you eat?

Do you eat more than once a day?

Why do you think your mind is any different? The problem is that your mind <u>has</u> to feed daily, just like your body, but if you don't give it the proper nourishment i.e. the positive thoughts you want it to feed on, then it is forced to take on whatever nourishment it can find, good or bad.

Let us talk some more about beliefs. What are beliefs? Well a belief is something you are strongly convinced about. Do people argue about their beliefs? Yes. Do you want to take sides when two people are arguing about something they both believe to be true? Probably not. Do people fight over their beliefs, thinking that theirs are right and the other person's must therefore be wrong? Yes. Do some people kill each other over beliefs? Yes. So would you agree that beliefs are very powerful and might get you to act in a certain way ... and therefore give you certain results? You bet!

What has this got to do with financial wealth creation? Well, imagine that you had a belief that goes something like this ... 'Rich people are all ... greedy' or 'rich people are all .... dishonest, selfish' etc. you can fill in the gap yourself, I am sure.

Well let me ask you something. Do you want to be greedy or dishonest or selfish? If the answer is no but you still think that wealthy people are, then you are linking something that you consider to be negative, to wealth. If you don't want to be greedy, dishonest, selfish etc. then you cannot be wealthy because in your mind, that is what wealthy people are ... and that's not you!

Can you see how a simple belief can stop you from becoming wealthy?

So what can you do? All you need to do is do the opposite of what you were doing before – start linking positive attributes to wealth. For example, is it possible that thousands of wealthy people around the world are actually honest giving people who contribute to society and create jobs and wealth for hundreds and thousands of other people, give to charity etc?

I hope you are agreeing with this because this is what I truly believe. You only need to think about Bill Gates who gave $19 billion to charity and Warren Buffett who gave $32 billion.

So what are your beliefs around money? (At the Wealth Workout™, we go through an exercise which allows you to pinpoint the beliefs that are stopping you from becoming wealthy. Would that be useful to you?)

Do you want to know the real kick in the head? Most people don't know

a) That beliefs are holding them back.

b) Which beliefs are holding them back.

But all you need to do is to look at the results (their finances, house, cars, boats – or lack of them) and you can immediately see that something is holding them back.

So now all we need to do is to uncover these beliefs. Here's how. Answer the following question. What are your beliefs about money? Take a moment to think about it.

What fears do you have about what it takes for you to make money – what is going to happen to you, your friends, your family etc. Take a moment to think about it.

Below are a few which come up the most:

- Wealth is not for people like me

It is for those other ... wealthy people

- Money changes people / I might become greedy

The idea that you turn into a self-obsessed monster is a common one.

- I'm too busy

Most people come home after a busy day making

someone else wealthy and are too tired to work on their own wealth creation and to take proper care of their families.

- Takes too long

There are people that will say it takes too long and at the end of saying this for years have nothing to show for it instead of starting now and reaping the rewards in years to come.

- I don't know where to start

A common one but unforgivable because never before have there been so many wealthy role models we can learn from if only we were willing to open our mouths and ask. You think you have it hard – try asking the first billionaires who was available for <u>them</u> to model ... no-one!

- I'm not interested in money – money is not important

What kind of person says this? Only a poor person, one that doesn't have any money might have to justify their situation in this way.

- Rich people are all ... greedy, dishonest, bad parents

Ok, this is getting silly now.

- When I win, someone else is losing

There is a pernicious lie making the rounds that there is not enough. Let me tell you that there is more than enough if you are willing to claim your share.

- I'm not good enough / intelligent / young / old enough

Why is it that some people will tell you that they are too young to create wealth, while another will tell you that they are too old? I have heard people say that the reason they have not created wealth is due to a lack of education, while others will firmly tell you that they are over-educated.

People have a whole list of reasons and justifications as to why they do not make things happen because it is easier to blame something, someone or a situation rather than take action.

- Fear of losing what I have now / when I make it

This is a common one, and while I can understand the fear of losing the money I have now (this is a typical fear of middle class who have something to lose), some people don't take any action because they actually believe that when they make the money the tax man will take it, people will want hand-outs, they feel it as a burden and finally they might lose it all! This has all happened in their minds before even taking a single step towards making the money and stops them dead in their tracks. They haven't even made it and in their mind they have already lost it - can you see how powerful the mind is?

- Fear of winning! / My friends won't like me anymore

This is a big one for people whether they realise it or not – the biggest fear is of succeeding because as human beings we want to be part of a group and not be rejected. Imagine making money and suddenly people around you started treating you differently. Some people would rather play it small than lose the affection of their friends, family etc. By the way, it is their belief that they will lose the affection of their friends and family, it may not be the reality at all. And so they decide to play small.

Who are you to play small and not shine your light to illuminate the world?

So these were a short list of some of the most common beliefs I hear. Did any of them resonate with you, either because you thought they were silly or because you think you might be suffering from one of them?

Where do these Beliefs come from?

When we are born we need to learn to eat, talk and walk and so our brains are made to soak up every bit of information like a sponge. This is how we learn. So from the moment we are born we are not only open to the influences of people and things, we are actually soaking it up. All our senses, our eyes, ears, touch, smell and taste are straining to get this information into our brains. So we learn through what we saw, heard, felt, smelt and tasted.

The analogy of a computer downloading software is a good one - imagine your head being like a neck-top computer, downloading the programmes and then running them in our minds. These programmes make us react in a certain way to situations and give us results based on our reactions. That is what people mean when they say, "Thoughts become things".

Some people run the same patterns their entire life based on the beliefs that were handed down to them. Yes, we are saying that it is unlikely that the beliefs you have are even your own! This is where they most likely came from:

- Your Family

In your formative years, from age 0-7, you spend most of your time with your family. No wonder then that the apple rarely falls far from the tree. Did you ever hear, see or experience your parents arguing about money? Did you ever hear any of the following comments from anyone in your family when you asked them for money? "Do you think money grows on trees?" / "Do you think I am made of money?" / "What do you think I am, a bank?" Most people will acknowledge that this 'lack' programming happened at some stage while they were young.

- School

Did you go to a school where you wore a uniform and you were basically told to sit down, shut up, listen and repeat what you were told? This type of forced discipline taught us to be like everyone else and not to think outside of the box and entrepreneurially. That's why most people get a job. And that's why most people end their lives in debt.

Did they ever tell you to write 'lines' as a punishment? "I must not talk in class. I must not talk in class." This is massive programming because something that is repeated often enough (and with enough emotion) works miracles on the Unconscious.

- Friends

Do you have friends that get you down? Instead of helping you they try to keep you where you are not because they don't want you to succeed per se, but because of how it will make them look and feel if you succeed. It will make them look and feel bad and they don't like feeling bad. Other friends just don't want you to change because they like you the way you are and don't want to 'lose you'.

Imagine coming to a financial wealth creation seminar. What would your 'friends' say about that? Will they start to discourage you, laugh, and sneer or get defensive? Notice their reaction when you are trying to better your position in life.

- Media

If you believe you escaped the programming brought to you by your family, school and friends (and that's just not possible because you are just the sum total of everything you saw, heard and felt), then the media will finish you off.

If you are reading a newspaper with all their negative focus designed to sell you the newspaper, you are only really using one sense – your eyes / visual. If you are listening to the radio you are only using your ears / auditory.

But when you are watching television / film you are using 3 senses: You are watching a film (visual), you are listening to the surround sound effects (auditory) and you are getting emotional as you react to the plot (kinaesthetic). When you are using 2-3 sense you are hypnotised. For example, have you ever cried during a film? Why?! It was just an actor, right? We get emotional because as we are hypnotised our Conscious reasoning mind is disabled and our Unconscious takes over. Our Unconscious does not understand the difference between what is real and what isn't and so you react emotionally, taking on a double dose of programming. I mean just listen to the word programme – television channels openly admit they are programming us – what programme are you watching – BBC, ITV or channel 4?

I could go on about the many different films where the baddies are the wealthy people and the poor people are the goodies, like Spiderman, Titanic etc. but a particularly bad wealth programme was aired in the 80s called Dallas. If I hum the theme tune, most people would be able to finish humming it – and programming doesn't work!? Well this was all about a rich oil family in Dallas, Texas and we flocked to watch it every week because we wanted to know how the Rich live – we lapped it up. The main person we loved to hate – notice the use of emotions, which just increases the programming – was JR Ewing. JR was a drunk, he was unfaithful to his wife, in fact she was probably the only woman he didn't sleep with, he was out to screw everyone in business, so he was dishonest and guess what, he was incredibly wealthy.

This programme taught us that wealthy people are drunks, unfaithful and dishonest. It is probably the most vicious anti-rich programming available and entire generations lapped it up eagerly.

- Organised religion

This is one I am not going to get sucked into because the beliefs around religion are so strong. Some religions tell you that you are a sinner and not worthy right from the start – in fact we have had the 'fear of God' programmed into us from an early age. Can you imagine trying to become wealthy when you constantly feel as if you are not worthy and basically a sinner?

And don't even get me started about the one I hear the most – money is the sin of all evil, which is a misquote from the bible, which says, "the Love of money is the sin of all evil." Now I don't know about you but I want the lifestyle that money can give me, not the money itself.

If you need more convincing about this let me assure you that the Vatican and the organised Church is one of the most wealthy and powerful Institutions on the planet. I am not just talking about the Vatican and its priceless masterpieces on show in the Vatican Museum nor the vast unseen subterranean football-sized halls filled with priceless treasures. I am talking about the millions of real estate / churches it has around the world and also the most priceless wealth of all – it has the hearts and minds of millions of people around the earth to do its bidding.

The way to control people is through ignorance, fear and poverty, not education, self esteem and wealth. But when you go back to the bible, the first personal development book ever written, the bible abounds with advice on how to become financially wealthy and to look after your finances.

Learn how to create the beliefs that make us money

So how do we create some beliefs that instead of taking us away from wealth actually bring us closer to it? This is a simple process outlined below:

First, you need to acknowledge that maybe you are not perfect. Are you willing to admit that? I only ask because a lot of people don't want to change – they want their situation or the results they are getting to change without changing themselves. This is impossible.

Are you willing to admit that maybe there might be a belief or two which were programmed into you years ago which might still be holding you back? Poor people don't believe they need to change – they prefer that everyone else changes and so they stay poor. Poor people are basically 'know it alls'. They know someone down the pub who heard from someone else that these things don't work. They don't like to surround themselves with people who know more than them because it makes them feel bad about themselves and 'the card they have been dealt'.

Wealthy people on the other hand are the opposite – they are 'learn it alls'. They are not afraid of surrounding themselves with people who know more than them because they know they can learn from them and get ahead. They actually seek out people who know more than them and can help them. Poor people would avoid doing this.

The second step is to find out what these beliefs are. Remember that sometimes we don't know what belief is holding us back – all we know by looking at the results of our actions is that we don't have as many 'fruits of our labour' as we would like. So we know the beliefs need to be changed but we don't know which ones.

At the Wealth Workout™, we take you through this process so we know exactly which beliefs we need to be working on.

The third step is to get rid of the belief that doesn't serve us. Again this is a specific process we go through at the Wealth Workout™ using a variety of techniques designed specifically for this purpose.

The fourth step is to replace these old beliefs with a new one of our choosing. If you just eliminate the old belief, you have created a vacuum that needs filling. Remember that the mind needs feeding on a daily basis and while it takes on new programmes the Unconscious can't distinguish good and bad, right or wrong because that's the job of your Conscious. Before you know it, you have replaced the belief you eliminated with the same belief, one that is equally as bad or perhaps one that is even worse!

So what belief can we choose to replace it with? One way of doing it is to take the exact opposite belief to the old one. In our research we have found 14 separate ways in which wealthy people think as opposed to poor people. This list forms the basis of our process at the Wealth Workout™.

The fifth step is to understand that it has taken years of continuous programming to form the beliefs you have now and to make you who you are. It is unusual to be able to change this within a few seconds – but it is possible. There are certain significant emotional events which will instantly change your beliefs. An example of this is usually when something bad happens i.e. someone you love gets seriously ill or even dies. Suddenly you realise that life is a gift and worth living to the full. This has a massive and at times lasting impact on your beliefs, and therefore your behaviours and therefore your results.

Normally however, new beliefs need a certain amount of conditioning and repetition to really build up a belief that sticks. At the Wealth Workout™ we use a variety of tools and techniques to speed up the process. After this, you will still be required to do some exercises and although they take only seconds, they do need to be done every day ... if you want to create financial wealth in your life. But like I say, it takes just seconds.

Wow, we have completed the first step: **Discover what is holding us back and deal with it.** This is by far the biggest step and most important step. How do I know this for sure? Because the majority of people don't think it is important ... and the majority of people are poor.

Let us now to go the next step.

I like thinking big, if you're going to be thinking, you might as well think big.

Donald Trump

2: Find our financial vision and purpose

Financial Vision

Are you sick and tired of hearing about how you need to 'know what you really want' and to 'set goals'? Why do the experts always go on about these things? Probably because they work!

Here I am talking about your financial vision. Most people don't know what they want. But they know what they don't want. This is a good place to start – just imagine the opposite of what you don't want and go from there.

How can you ever get to where you want to go if you don't know what it looks like and where it is? But it gets worse. Imagine just going with the flow and letting life lead you in a certain direction. If you take just 2 steps in the 'wrong' direction in the opposite way to your financial vision, how many steps will you need to take to get you to where you would have been, had you known the direction of your financial vision? The answer is not 2, that would just get you back to your starting point. The answer is in fact 4, twice the number of steps. But it gets even worse – what has the effort been? Two steps away, two steps to the starting point and another 2 steps in the right direction. In other words 3 times the effort and think of the energy and time wasted.

That is why it makes so much financial sense to do what the masses will never do – and that is to take time out to really think about what you want financially: what it looks like, sounds like, feels like, smells like and tastes like to be financially wealthy for you. In other words, we are talking about slowing down in order to go faster. In his brilliant book, the 7 Habits of Highly Successful People, Stephen Covey tells us to "begin with the end in mind." He describes how people in their haste to do things rush up a ladder to get to the top. Instead of feeling elated at getting to the top they realise that they have spent valuable time and energy climbing up a ladder which was leaning against the wrong house. You can never get this time back, it is gone forever, so I would say to you again: "Slow down in order to go faster" or as one of my secretaries told me once, "Less haste and more speed". She was right. The Wealth Workout™ allows you the time to do exactly that – find out what it is you want in a supportive environment away from the hassles and demands of everyday life.

Financial Purpose

But there is more. Most people don't have a vision but even the ones that do are unlikely to get to it if they do not have a big enough purpose. What is a purpose? It is your why – WHY do you want to be wealthy. So people have a vision and work hard but at some stage they don't want to go on. One day they will wake up and think, "Why am I doing this again – it is so hard". They then quit when success was just around the corner.

This section gives you the secret to success so please pay attention.

In fact I would go as far as to say that the reason you haven't achieved what you want and deserve is because your WHY is not big enough. If I were you I would create a big purpose as soon as possible. You may have heard of Napoleon Hill who spent 25 years interviewing the richest people, both Millionaires and Billionaires at a time when that was still a big deal, to find out what made them successful. On his deathbed, Napoleon Hill was asked out of all the things he discovered, what were the most important? And without hesitating he said that there were two that he felt were head and shoulders above the rest. The second we will discuss later, but the first one he said was "To have a Purpose, a goal that is bigger than you!" Read that sentence again. Tell me what you think are the most important words in that sentence. Most people will say 'goal' or bigger" but when you put it together, "a goal that is bigger than you" is where it all starts.

Here's why.

If you make it about yourself, you are going to fall prey to all the limiting beliefs you have about how you are not good enough, not clever enough, not a good enough presenter, not enough knowledge, education etc. In other words, you believe that you need to be perfect to succeed, which is just pure rubbish. Rubbish or not, they are your beliefs and they can stop you dead in your tracks. So the key is not to focus on you, but rather make your project, your cause, your PURPOSE about something bigger than you. Make it about someone else, about the charity, the children, the orphanage, about your customers, about your mission etc. anything but not about yourself.

Why are you here on this earth? What is your purpose? Wouldn't you like to find out? Don't you think it is our duty to find out? I can share our purpose with you: we are here to help as many people around the world create financial wealth for themselves and their families. That is why we are here, that is the legacy we have decided to leave. We started with the stock market and realised that people need a much more fundamental education – one that isn't taught in school. And the result of keeping us in the dark and depriving us of much needed financial education, or financial literacy as Robert Kiyosaki calls it, is that we are a nation in debt. We now teach this information in schools. It isn't about me – it is about our mission and purpose to educate people financially, so they can live a lifestyle of abundance and joy.

What is your Purpose for getting up in the morning that makes you want to jump out of bed with joy? Let us help you find yours so that you can lead a life of purpose, joy and fulfilment. Don't make it about yourself because if you do, you could lead a life of emptiness and despair and feeling unfulfilled. I wouldn't wish that on my worst enemies.

Remember this: You will do things for other people you wouldn't do for yourself. Parents know this – they will go without food if they think their children aren't going to be fed. They buy them things even if it means going without themselves.

I can get anyone to do something by giving them enough leverage over themselves, i.e. having enough of a reason

WHY they should do it. Imagine asking someone who is scared of public speaking to come up on stage and talk about a subject they know nothing about. Would they do it? Probably not. I mean, there is even a book called, *...and Death came Third* because people fear public speaking more than death.

But if you informed that same person that their child was sick and the only way of saving it was for them to talk in front of an audience on a subject they know nothing about because everyone in the audience would donate £10 which would raise sufficient funds for the top surgeon in the world to fly in to perform the life saving operation, do you think they would do it? Would you do it? When can I start, right? The point is that the person has been given a massive reason why, a purpose to do it.

The only reason you aren't where you want to be is because your purpose is not big or juicy enough. Juice it up, make it big, bright and wonderful and you will rocket towards your goals ... and did I mention, don't make it about you.

Just £2.50 a day could be worth £5,000,000 to you over a lifetime if you just knew how.

Marcus de Maria

3: Plan for wealth

Oh dear oh dear oh dear. We don't learn planning at school, let alone financial planning. I wonder how many people reading this have a financial plan which shows them where they are today (this is called your Net Worth), the year they become financial independent or financially free and lastly how to speed up the process? My guess is not that many. Why - because of our limiting beliefs around money and also because we were never taught how to do so.

It is unlikely that you were taught by your parents if they never planned themselves.

Let's test a theory of mine – I think you know the importance of planning. See if you can finish the following sentence:

If you don't plan to be rich then you're planning to be .... poor

If you don't have your own plan, you will become part of .... someone else' plan

And the one that everyone knows:

If you fail to plan, you plan to .... fail

So you know how important it is to plan right? I mean, no builder, not even Donald Trump himself would say, "Hey guys, we have built so many buildings, we know what we are doing, so let's forget about planning, let's just start building." It wouldn't happen because not only do they plan but every plan is detailed to the nearest millimetre, isn't it? Otherwise half-way through building when they forget to put windows and doors in, they are going to have to tear the whole thing down.

So you know how important planning is, right? Then why don't you have a plan? You have just admitted that it would be crazy not to have a plan and in the same breath admit that you don't have one?

Let's ask a better question - do you want to have a financial plan? If the answer is YES, read on.

We have spent a lot of time, effort and expense coming up with a financial tool that allows you to put in your data online and which then allows you to work out your current financial situation. Do you know your monthly outgoings? A lot of people do know this but they don't include the weekly cash they take out which just seems to disappear. I remember one particular gentleman tell me that he didn't need to work out his monthly expenditure because he knew it. I asked him politely to do it anyway just to check and he was out by, wait for it ... 60%. Where does all the money you spend go to? Well it goes on things like the odd coffee here, a sandwich there and a drink over here.

There is even a name for it – it is called the Latte Factor. This is where you go into your local coffee outlet to buy some hot black burnt water. As you wait in the queue you are tempted by a croissant or a snack for later. As you pay, it doesn't cost that much - maybe £2.50. But this is exactly where the danger lays – this 'not so expensive' £2.50 a day over 50 years is actually worth close to £45,000. Could you do with an extra £45,000?

And this isn't even the point. If you would have taken that £2.50 a day and put it into a FTSE (Financial Times Stock Exchange) tracker, it would have turned that money onto £2,000,000 in the same time frame. Yes you heard correctly, this is no joke. I am totally serious when I tell you that every time you pay for a half pack of cigarettes or buy a coffee and a croissant, you are taking a massive chunk out of £2,000,000. This is due to the power of compound growth, something I am going to explain in more detail later.

Don't get me wrong – if you want to spend the money go right ahead – but do it with the knowledge of what you are doing, not out of ignorance. You can now no longer blame your parents for not teaching you, wave an angry finger at the Government, your partner or anyone else but one person alone ... you. Your financial future lies entirely in your hands, and we can help you speed up that process. But back to the financial planner, the best bit is yet to come.

The financial planner allows you to answer questions like, how much money do you earn on a yearly basis, how much tax do you pay, what is the rate of inflation etc. These are all things you can find out from your accountant or financial advisor – if not, we can help. Then there are just 4 questions you need to answer.

1. What do you guesstimate will be your percentage increase in earnings over the next few years? Most people don't know but we will put a figure which is above inflation, say 5%. Because if you are not getting a pay increase which is above inflation then you are actually getting paid less every year! So let's stay with 5% increase a year.

2. What percentage of your income are you committed to saving and investing on an annual basis? At this stage I tend to get some blank stares. "Me, save and invest"? Yes you, because this is the only way to become wealthy if you aren't going to win it

via the lottery (fat chance), steal it or marry into it. Some people tell me that they do save and quote a number like £300 - £400 a month. This is good but it needs to be a percentage of what you earn, for example 10% of your net (after tax) salary is the minimum you should start with. The reason is that as your income increases, so will the number if it is a percentage. £300-£400 of £3,500 is not the same as £300 - £400 of £6,000.

I have had two separate couples tell me that they save around 50% of everything that they earn. Wow. And no, they didn't have any children. But they had a big Purpose – one of them was saving up for a new house and the other for a wedding. That Purpose thing is quite powerful.

I think a good place to start is to save and invest 10%, minimum.

3. The next question is what percentage return can you get on your combined investments? In other words when you take your 10% and invest it what annual percentage return can you make on your investments? Now most people tell me they make just 4% in the bank or 6% in a high yield bank account. But that is not what I am talking about – I

am talking about stocks & shares, property in the UK, property abroad, someone else's business and other investments.

I always have a few people in the room who know roughly what they are getting and it can be 20% - 50% a year upwards. I usually guess that this is through property and it usually is, although sometimes it is in the stock market. Very rarely it is selling products through Ebay or internet marketing. The only reason you might not be making this kind of a return is because you have not yet had the education. We can plug that gap for you. I am going to put 12% a year in there for you. Sounds high? It isn't. The reason is that since 1969 the average FTSE return has been 12.4%. So if you just stuck some money in without doing anything else, including the downward 'bear' markets, including the crash of 1987, including the fall when the planes hit the Twin Towers in September 2001, the average return over time is still 12.4%. Just imagine what would have happened if you had put more money in every time those scenarios happened and waited for the inevitable rise? Wooah Marcus, you are giving away far too much already, let's continue with this first.

4. Finally, would you agree that there are high yield bank accounts where if you were to invest your money (not your current accounts), you could get upwards of 6% a year or even more? Imagine this scenario. The year you decide to stop working and live off the fruits of your labour you sell everything you own, maybe even downsize your house and you put it into 2-3 different bank accounts (just in case) and you live off that 6% return. In other words, you just go to the bank once a year and take off the 6% growth (you will have to pay tax on it) and wait another year for another 6% growth. Your capital always stays the same. Sound good?

Put all those figures onto the online financial planner and hey presto, you suddenly know the year you can stop working or you have a choice whether you want to continue or not. That year is called your Financial Independence Year. Would you like to know what year that is for you? Most people run around like headless chickens trying to make money. If you stop them and ask them what they are doing this for, they look at you with a blank stare or a "you're a moron" look. Because most people mistakenly think they will stop working when they are 60-65. WRONG! You will have to carry on working if you don't have enough money set aside. Isn't the retirement age being put back? And we are all going to live longer so we need even more money.

There is an example financial planner on the next page. It tells you your financial independence date – the date you are independent from work. You have the choice. Ok, so how much money would you like to earn from that 6% i.e. how much money do you want to collect once a year from the bank? This is passive money and you won't ever have to do anything else at all. Most people tend to answer at the around £100,000 mark.

Let's take a look at the financial planner. Someone has put in all their financial data; how much they earn, save, and invest etc. According to the 3rd column – Pre Tax annual income from your Critical Mass, you will receive £108,975 (before tax) by 2025 which is in 16 years time.

Can you see the amount of financial control this gives you? Before you didn't have a clue what you were working towards. You had some notion about retiring at 60-65 and the thought of needing millions but you had no real idea until now. The Financial Freedom Calculator tells you exactly when you can stop working, if you want to.

But the best is still to come. Now that you know the date you can give up work – something you never knew before, what can you do now?

	YOUR WEALTH			ANNUAL INCOME	
Year	"CRITICAL MASS" End of Year Capital Invested	Pre Tax Annual Income from Critical Mass	Pre Tax Monthly Income from Annual Pre Tax Income	Annual Income	Annual Savings
	£	£	£	£	£
2009	244,193	14,652	1,221	49,350	4,935
2010	274,599	16,476	1,373	51,818	5,182
2011	308,619	18,517	1,543	54,408	5,441
2012	345,155	20,709	1,726	57,129	5,713
2013	390,952	23,457	1,955	59,985	5,999
2014	442,586	26,555	2,213	62,984	6,298
2015	500,798	30,048	2,504	66,134	6,613
2016	566,421	33,985	2,832	69,440	6,944
2017	636,873	38,212	3,184	72,912	7,291
2018	726,170	43,570	3,631	76,558	7,656
2019	827,734	49,664	4,139	80,386	8,039
2020	943,251	56,595	4,716	84,405	8,441
2021	1,074,641	64,478	5,373	88,626	8,863
2022	1,216,960	73,018	6,085	93,057	9,306
2023	1,390,304	83,418	6,952	97,710	1,954
2024	1,588,832	95,330	7,944	102,595	2,052
2025	1,816,253	108,975	9,081	107,725	2,154
2026	2,076,823	124,609	10,384	113,111	2,262
2027	2,360,435	141,626	11,802	118,767	2,375
2028	2,699,206	161,952	13,496	124,705	1,247
2029	3,087,498	185,250	15,437	130,940	1,309
2030	3,532,632	211,958	17,663	137,487	1,375
2031	4,043,016	242,581	20,215	144,362	1,444
2032	4,598,145	275,889	22,991	151,580	1,516

Can you guess what it is?

The answer is, now you can speed up the process. Before, without any measurements there was nothing to speed up, but now we know that there are 4 things you can speed up. What are they?

1. The amount of money you earn. How can you get more than a 5% increase a year? There are so many different ways, but one of them might be asking for a bigger raise. Come on, if you don't ask you won't get and if you don't ask, your boss may not respect you. For example, I will not give a raise to any of my employees if they don't ask – do you know why? Because if they don't ask then they obviously don't think they are worth it. If on the other hand they believe they are worth it, I will take note. I will set them some targets and milestones and if they achieve them they get a raise. Win-win all the way.

   Here is another idea – making a part-time hobby or business pay for you. Can you speak English? Well you can certainly read it if you understand what I am writing. Could you teach some wealthy foreigners English or even help them practice speaking English over the phone? How much can you charge for that an hour? What if you charged £10? What if you did 10 hours a week and made an extra £100 a week? This doesn't sound like much but an extra £400 a month can make ALL the difference. Could you pay off your debts, could you save more, would it pay for some of the shopping?

Now what do you think happens to the Financial Freedom Calculator when we put in the new figures? The answer is simple – you can start retiring even earlier, years earlier.

2. Could you save/ invest more of your income? How close to the 50% that both those couples managed to do could you come to? Do you really need to buy all those 'Latte factor' things like cable TV, subscriptions you don't use, coffee, snacks and drinks, cigarettes etc.

   Could you change some branded goods so you save on those? Could you buy in bulk at Lidl or Aldi instead of buying small packets at the corner shop? Could you make your own sandwiches, costing you 50 pence instead of £2.95 – they are tastier, healthier and you know what's inside them. The list is endless.

Now what do you think happens to the Financial Freedom Calculator when we put in the new figures? The answer is simple – you can start retiring even earlier.

This is much more exciting than mere budgeting – this is about speeding up your financial freedom date.

3. What about the % return on investments? We put them in at 12% because of the historic performance of the stock market index, but if you wanted more we can deliver on that too. How about 15%. That would make quite a big difference, I can tell you. Again there are several ways in which you can do this. One is the strategy we teach at the Wealth Workout™, which has a return of 15% a year. It is a variation on the old Dogs of the Dow strategy which, while popular, is not working at the moment due to low dividends. Don't worry if you didn't understand that, but rest assured we have something that works, that's all that matters.

   You can make a lot more than 15% on property in the UK and abroad. We are getting some amazing discounts on properties (27%) right now. At the time of writing, overseas property is the way to go for us personally due to the strong growth prospects abroad. We can give you more information about property in the UK and abroad, and the Wealth Workout™ helps to frame it all.

Now what do you think happens to the Financial Freedom Calculator when we put in the new figures? The answer is simple – you can start retiring even earlier.

4. Finally would it be possible to find a high yield savings account at 6.3% instead of 6%? The answer is let's find out because again if we can get an extra .3% a year then this makes a difference to the FFC – and you can start retiring even earlier.

The great thing about the Financial Freedom Calculator is that when you look at it on a quarterly basis and your net worth has not changed, it motivates you into action. But if it has changed for the better, it motivates you even more because you think – "what else can I do?"

Would you like to get your hands on our Financial Freedom Calculator? You bet you need to, for yourself, your family and you friends. It is an awesome tool which for the first time gives you the financial control you want for yourself and your loved ones.

A man is not defeated when he's finished;
he's finished when he quits.

Richard Nixon

4: Understand what money is and attract it into our lives

Before we get carried away with the making of money and living the lifestyle of our dreams, we need to know what money actually is. How can you get it if you don't understand what it is?

Is money just a coin or piece of paper? Is it a form of barter and exchange? This is what most people think, but I am going to ask you to look at it differently. In my opinion it is a mixture of three things, all as important as each other:

1. Perceived Value: Money is nothing but a reflection of the perceived value you give to people around you.

   Go ahead and read that sentence again. If you are not delivering what people around you consider to be value, they are not going to pay you. If on the other hand you deliver what they consider to be value, you will make money.

   Most people do it the other way around. Rather than find out what people want, they spend time holed up coming up with an invention. After several years they emerge holding the best mousetrap ever only to find that ... no-one wants it. Oh dear. I guess asking a few people (market research) might have helped.

Notice that it is not just about value but about 'perceived' value. You can think that you are adding a lot of value (nurses, teachers etc.) who I personally think add so much value, but our country does not value their services and so they are not very well paid. I would argue that they should be the most highly paid people but the market's perception does not agree with me.

Please note that this is the same whether you are employed or not. If you are self-employed then you need to add the most value to the customer. If you are employed then the customer comes second – your first priority is your boss.

This is the first part. You also need to add the following:

2. How CREATIVE can you be with the value you add?

Why is it that people around you are earning more money, getting salary raises, getting promoted etc. Are they better than you? No. Are they more intelligent than you? Nope. Are they better looking than you? Definitely not! The only reason is that they are being more creative with the value they add.

The example I like to give is in the service industry. There are lots of coaches and consultants out there, so let's take success or life coaches. For this example, we are going to assume that all the coaches mentioned all have the same level of competency. Imagine coach A is a very good coach, in fact he is above average and is proud of the results he gets for his clients. He believes that his results speak louder than words and so relies on referrals. Fair enough. Coach B decides to be creative. So he records the call with the client so that they client can listen to it again and again and get further distinctions every time. Does this cost a lot of money or effort to do? No. Is it creative with the value added? Yes. Coach C does this as well, but also offers a CD on how to achieve your goals. Coach D does the same but in addition has written a report on "The 7 Mistakes to avoid when hiring a coach and how to get the most out of your coaching sessions". Coach E does all this but also has a website with a free members section where people are able to get downloads.

These were written not by Coach E but experts in their fields and add massive creative value. Coach F has written a book. It is an OK book, not great, but it has his picture on the front cover and positions him as an absolute expert, head and shoulders above the other coaches.

Now here is a question for you. Which of the 5 coaches do you think is able to command the most fees and get the most clients, even though they all have the same level of coaching skills? The answer should be no surprise to you, it is ... Coach F.

Think about your industry and think about what all the successful people in that industry are doing. I bet the list is long and will keep you busy for quite a while. If not, then think outside of your industry. If you don't think it applies, ask a better question, like "How could it apply to me and my industry?" Then get moving on it.

There is not a single industry where this cannot be done.

Two down and one to go – the last part of the equation is:

3. What is your unique talent?

    What is the one thing you were put on this earth for? What are you passionate about? Is there one thing that you can do until the cows come home – when you look at your watch and it is past midnight. You thought it was much earlier you were having so much fun. You didn't realise it but you were so in your flow that you literally warped time and time stood still for you.

    If you are not sure, what could it be?

    Because your talent, the thing you were uniquely put on this earth for, is your currency. Find it. Expand on it, develop it, and get out there and make your fortune with it.

A lot of people say to me that their hobbies could not make them money. I absolutely beg to disagree. One lady said that she could not see how her dancing hobby could make her money. You've got to be kidding me. I mean where do you start on that one – DVDs, books, reports, videos, group dancing lessons, small group dancing lessons, 1-1 lessons, coaching, mentoring, speed-learning in one weekend etc.

I am not saying that she will make a £million out of it but she will make enough for a decent lifestyle and if you get paid doing something you love ... now that is real wealth. Talking of a million, there was recently a story about a 19-year-old who had made a £1 million out of a hobby. Picture yourself at the local big supermarket looking at the rows upon rows of jams and marmelades. As you look at them can you see an obvious market niche or opportunity? I mean they have thought of everything already, right? Wrong. In actual fact this 19-year-old made £1 million out of a recipe which his grandmother had come up with and made it organic.

Now why didn't *I* think of that?!

Money is nothing but flow-like Energy

Let me tell you something, which I would like you to write on your forehead ... there is no such thing as a lack of money. There is so much money in this world, enough to go around. In fact, I once read that if all the money in the world were to be handed out equally to everyone, then everyone would be a millionaire. No, it is not a lack of money that is the problem. The problem is a lack of ideas (and acting on those ideas).

Think about this for a moment. Imagine you were back in 2000. The dotcom bubble has just burst. Dotcom companies are worthless. If you were faced with the number one search engine in the world, Yahoo, would you want to take it on? They absolutely dominated their industry back then. But that is exactly what a young group did and set up a company called Google. There were already many search engines competing – do you remember Lycos, Ask Jeeves and Alta Vista – but as crazy as it sounds they thought they could do it differently. The result? Google is the number one and worth billions. What about ideas such as social networking site Myspace – worth billions again? What about the idea of having videos put on a website and calling it YouTube? What about Facebook? Why didn't we think of that?

My grandparents wouldn't have understood these internet companies, because they don't understand where the real, hard value is. Some of them don't even make enough money to warrant such a high valuation. Unfortunately my grandparents have both passed away, bless them, but my grandparents died penniless, having rented the same house all their lives. They could have bought that house several times over, but they never did and didn't have an asset to their name. It is because they didn't understand the basics of wealth creation.

They needed a Wealth Workout™, but it is too late for them.

The fact is that we used to live in the 'work hard' era. Then it was the 'work smart' era. Now it is the 'creative thought' era. People are literally making up the rules as they go along, redefining industries. Just before he died I showed my grandad the internet. He found it amazing. We are living in the era of 'creative thought' and this is what Alchemy is all about. The alchemists tried to turn base metals into gold. This can never happen. But if you use your imagination and build something with earth, like bricks, and use metal to erect a building, then you can turn nothing into a block of flats and make your gold that way. By having these ideas, and putting them into action, people are creating ideas literally out of thin air.

Some more examples, and please note your reaction when you read them. Have you seen some of the things that are being sold on Ebay? Once they had a plaster cast of the poop of Tom Cruise's first child. Another example: A Celebrity was having a party and being a celebrity everyone received a little cake with her face on it. The next day it was selling on Ebay – guess for how much?

You'll never guess ...

Give up?

£6,000

Now when we discussed this at the Wealth Workout™, I remember one guy banging the table in frustration and shouting, "Well what the F%$!K is money then?" and he had a massive breakthrough right there and then, because money is not tangible, it is intangible, like energy.

That's right, money is creative energy.

I'd like you to imagine money being like flow – flowing around your house, your office, everywhere you are, it is all around you. The only challenge is that we tend to stop that flow and allow it to stagnate because of several things. I won't go into all of them now, but here are a few examples of the things that block your flow:

<u>Being untidy</u>: do you have a house which is full of 'clutter'. Your wardrobes are full of clothes you haven't worn in ages and are not likely to wear again? Are your drawers full of objects and 'things' you don't use? Are they a mess? The older we get the more we collect lots of different 'things' that people give to us, or we buy on impulse. But if they do not serve a purpose, or are not there to make you feel good, then they are quite simply blocking your flow. Money cannot flow to you.

What about your desk? This is the place where you create your money. Is it tidy or is it covered with piles of paper? Be honest ... Again if this is the case then money cannot flow to you. It is because unconsciously you are aware of all the other projects on your desk and it impossible to fully focus on the one project you are doing which is going to make you money. Let's look at this in more detail.

Being unfocused: I am going to exaggerate this a little but see if the following description rings a bell. You are at your desk – you have decided that you are going to focus on the one project that will make you money. As you start to work, you realise how messy your desk is. So you stop working and start tidying up. As you do so, you see a piece of paper and it is an interesting article, so you start to read it. After you finish, you still have the tidying up to do, but you realise that you should be working so you put everything into one pile and continue your work. Nothing has been achieved apart from wasting your time.

Suddenly out of the corner of your eye you see a scrap of paper reminding you to ring someone urgently. Although this has nothing to do with your money-making project, it is urgent so you go ahead and ring. The conversation takes longer than you thought but at least it is finished. A sense of achievement envelopes you so you restart your work with renewed vigour. It is at around that time you suddenly have a craving for a cup of tea or coffee. This takes you a little longer because you meet a co-worker and have a quick chat. Nothing has been achieved apart from wasting your time.

Suddenly you have an urge to check your emails - after all, the last time you checked was a full hour ago. You want to stay disciplined so you only spend a few seconds on each email until you get to one with an interesting link which takes you off to another site. The things you see there give you lots of ideas about something completely unrelated to the money-making activity you are supposed to be working on. After 10 minutes or so – it isn't that long – you restart your work. Just as you do, the telephone rings. You pick it up, which is what you must do when the telephone rings. The conversation, although unscheduled, takes just 10 minutes – it's really not a long time. Nothing has been achieved apart from wasting your time.

As you restart your project, someone pops their head into your workspace and asks, "Do you have a minute?" Of course you do, it isn't like you are busy creating wealth or anything, and for some reason the discussion doesn't take 'a minute' at all, but 15 minutes plus another 10 minutes or so getting another hot drink while you are talking, because that saves time. You look at your watch and cannot believe it – it is almost lunchtime. The problem is that you now have other projects that you need to start working on. Best to have an early lunch and restart later. Just then your mobile rings and without thinking you answer it because that is what people do when mobiles ring.

I know that the above description was a little bit exaggerated, but do you find yourself doing this – where you end the day and wonder where it all went and what was achieved? Picking up the same pieces of paper you still haven't read or made a decision on? Most people will never achieve real wealth in this way.

Being disorganised: I have visited people at their homes where they have piles of unopened envelopes stashed away, with the words, "Southend-on-Sea", written on them. This is where credit card companies are based. When I asked about them, they replied, "Oh you don't want to worry about that". This is called putting your head in the sand like an Ostrich. People have bank accounts, stocks left to them by relatives, maybe even an ISA or two but because they don't understand it, they fear it. While I can understand this, it is important that all the information is placed into one folder if it is paper, or ideally an excel spreadsheet. You don't need to study it, just file it. The next step would be to look at it but that is another topic.

Reprogramme your Unconscious

Where we can help you in a very fundamental way to create wealth is to reprogramme the years of poverty thinking and turn your mind into a money magnet, where you are creating wealth instantly even while you sleep.

Your Unconscious mind is one of the most powerful mechanisms you have. It keeps your heart beating while you sleep, ensures you are breathing and all the vital functions your body needs to perform you are not even consciously aware of. Here are a few more examples:

Have you ever woken up in the middle of the night either with the most brilliant idea or remembering something you forgot to do? I mean, you were unconscious, sleeping, why did you wake up? It is because at some stage you asked yourself a question and during the night your Unconscious has the time to think about finding an answer and as soon as it does, hey presto, it wakes you up with the answer. Very powerful indeed.

Another example of the Power of your Unconscious is that you can literally programme it to do your bidding.

For example, do you know of anyone who can wake up at the same time every day without an alarm clock? How do they do that, after all they weren't conscious, they were unconscious, sleeping. That's the whole point. Somewhere along the line they programmed their Unconscious, which is taking care of you while you are sleeping and when it is time to wake up, it wakes you up.

What if there were a time to become wealthy? What if you programmed your Unconscious to deliver wealth for yourself day and night? Can it be done? Actually, it is the ONLY way to create wealth.

I am going to describe 5 stages of wealth which were researched by millionaires and billionaires. You tell me where you think you are:

> Stage 1: I'm not really interested in creating wealth. My parents were never really that focused on it and they were happy. People around me aren't that wealthy and they aren't too unhappy. And isn't it spiritual to be poor?

Or maybe you are closer to:

> Stage 2: I could be wealthy. I see other people doing things that achieve wealth and they don't seem

particularly unhappy about it. In fact, they seem quite happy.

Or maybe you are closer to:

Stage 3: I can be wealthy – I have made a few investments and seen that it is possible. People around me are doing ok.

Or maybe ...

Stage 4: I MUST become wealthy. There are no 'ifs' 'buts' or 'maybes'. It is like a white hot burning desire. Just get out of my way and give me the chance and I will prove it. We are talking massive action here.

The next stage is the best of all

Stage 5: I believe I am already wealthy. It is my birthright. It is only a matter of time before this belief manifests itself in the physical plane. But everything I desire, be it homes, cars, boats etc. are being built and assembled in factories around the world. And they are on their way to me right now. It is just a matter of time.

Where do you think you are on this spectrum 1 – 5?

Wherever you think you are, we have found that you are usually one stage behind what you thought.

This last stage 5 is where I need to get you as soon as possible because this is where all the riches lie. The moment you get that belief in yourself, that is the moment when it all starts happening for you. You had better be prepared for it when it happens.

Why is belief so important? Well in religion they call it faith, when prayers are answered and miracles happen. But let's just stay on the spiritual plane. Do you remember the film, *The Last Crusade* with Indiana Jones? Toward the end when the Nazi shoots Indie's father in the stomach to force Indie to go in to fetch the Holy Grail, Indie has three tasks he must complete. The first is about the 'humble man' and at that moment he kneels and misses being sliced in half by two huge discs. The second step is to spell Jehovah and he almost falls to his death.

The final task in to take the leap of faith. So Indie comes out of a narrow passage and before him there is nothing between him and the other end – just a sheer drop down into the abyss. He looks at the piece of paper again and reads "Take the leap of faith". He looks down again and just sees the big drop and can't believe that he is being asked to plunge to his death.

He hesitates, unwilling to commit himself but at that very moment, his friend Marcus Brody shouts to get him to hurry, because his father's wound is getting worse. So what does Indie get? A massive purpose, a reason why he must take the step, which is bigger than him. So he takes a big step, getting ready to plunge to his death and suddenly his feet touch something he can't see. The camera pans out to the side and suddenly we see what we could not see before ... an unseen path!

It is a fantastic moment because it reveals to us something that we have suspected all along. That there is a purpose why we are here, there is a path for us to tread if only we dared to do so, a path which is there if we believe in ourselves enough to take it. This is the absolute key to creating any type of success, including financial wealth – the ability to believe enough in yourself, and that whatever happens it will always be OK. Once you have this, your financial miracles start to happen.

So where are you on this path on scale 1-5?

The only way you can believe in yourself is to re-programme the many years of programming. Do you have a wealth consciousness or not? And I don't mean you saying to yourself that you want wealth – I mean what does your unconscious truly believe?

You either have a wealth consciousness or you don't. Let me repeat what we said at the beginning of this book, which was this – the financial results you are getting at the moment have only 20% to do with the 'skills' that you have. 80% is the wealth psychology and mindset i.e. your Unconscious has a huge role to play with that. So instead of allowing your former programming to deliver you poverty, how about we change the programming and allow your Unconscious to deliver wealth.

To re-programme your Unconscious can be done, but it requires specific training. We teach you precisely how to do it using this process described by millionaires and billionaires at the Wealth Workout™!

But you have to actually use it.

> *Genius is one percent inspiration, ninety-nine percent perspiration.*
>
> *Thomas Edison*

5: Understand financial concepts & the skills to create money

There are 5 steps to wealth

Step 1: Plan to reduce and remove debt.

Here I am talking about bad debt, like credit card debt – anything which you have spent money on with nothing to show for it, i.e. no assets. Bad debt is like a cancer eating away at you and you need to get rid of it as soon as possible. The Wealth Workout™ deals with creating wealth and as such does not focus on debt reduction, however we do have reliable partners who do. If you want some help with debt, please contact us at **debt@investment-mastery.com** and we will do our best to help you.

Step 2: Make more money.

It is important they you increase the amount of money coming in, whether this is through asking for a raise, earning some money on the side through getting an extra job, starting a new business or just helping someone out. The difference a few hundred pounds a week makes over the years is quite extraordinary. Most people don't realise this and so don't bother. A fundamental mistake.

While this is the simplest and most immediate way of making money, it is also the least leveraged i.e. it normally means exchanging your time for money. The best known of these is called Earned income or a J.O.B. Most wealth creation experts ridicule a J.O.B. as Just Over Broke or Just Our Bodies because it relies on you exchanging your time for money. The downside of this strategy is that you can only work 24 hours a day if you don't take time off to eat, sleep or wash and so have set an automatic ceiling on your wealth.

However, I tend to disagree because every one of these people probably started with a job themselves. This is where you learn and also manage to save enough to either buy assets or make that leap into opening up your own business. My advice – don't be in such a rush to leave your job. It gives you the chance to earn regular income while you spend evenings and weekends working on creating wealth.

We cover this in more detail at the Wealth Workout™.

Step 3: Making saving fun!

We have already spoken about some ideas around step 2, step 3 and step 4 when discussing the financial freedom calculator which I won't repeat here. What I will say is how important it is to make the process fun. You can set yourself a budget. Most people find that limiting and boring, but don't view it in this way. Why not get the whole family involved and have a competition on how much you can save.

It is critical to know WHY you are doing this so let me help you with some more concepts. The following is what we teach in schools around the UK. It is not how much you earn that is important, it is how much you keep. Who is going to be wealthier at the age of retirement – the person who earns £20,000 a year or the person who earns £200,000 a year? The answer is of course the person who saves the most to invest. The person who earns £200,000 a year but spends £205,000 is going to end up in debt, while the person who earns £20,000 but just invests a few pounds a day will be a multi-millionaire by the age of 65.

This extremely powerful information is just not taught anywhere but is critical to our wealth. Some more examples:

Did you know that an 18-year-old who saves just £1 a day (that's £30 a month), if they were to find a vehicle to make them 15% a year (we show you how to do that at the Wealth Workout™) will be worth £2,500,000 by the time they reach 65. Imagine that, just £1 a day. Anyone can do it.

What about someone who is closer to 40? They have to save £5 a day at 15% a year and at the age of 65 would be worth over £1 million.

So you can do it, no matter what your age. If you are older you simply need to either save more on a daily basis or get a higher rate of return or wait a little longer or a mixture of all three, but it is possible.

By talking about this we have already started incorporating steps 4 and 5 – investing it and compounding your money. This is where the magic comes in.

Step 4: Invest your time and money – get the money working for you

Passive Income

This is the idea of leverage and passive income, an incredibly exciting topic. Unfortunately when I say the words 'passive' most people want it without doing anything for it. There is no way you can gain passive income 'passively', it just doesn't work that way.

The idea of passive income is that you do something once and then get paid again and again. Here are some examples:

Buy-to-let property: did the property just appear from nowhere or did you have to source it, then give it a lick of paint, rip out the toilets etc.? Did you have to find the tenants and ensure they pay? Even if you have outsourced these tasks, which makes it truly passive, you really are involved in doing something before the passive element kicks in.

In this example it kicks in when the tenant either pays enough rent for you to be making income or pays enough rent for you to pay off your mortgage.

Network marketing: otherwise known as referral marketing, MLM etc, this is a way for you to sell a company's products that you like to other people and get income that way. This doesn't sound very passive until the next bit where you attract other people to do the same. They join under your organisation and sell products to their friends and families and you get a very small 'override' on anything you do. This is a 3-5 year game plan and don't let anyone tell you any different. I know several people making a fortune in this way but they paid their dues up front. They worked it hard. Nothing wrong with that but the real passive element comes later.

Intellectual Property: the idea here is to write a book or create something like an invention once and then get paid royalties again and again. Music is another example of this.

E-books and other e-products: with the internet you can literally tap into a world-wide market and have people buy something you wrote only once. Another idea is to choose someone else's product and sell that to the public for a 50% commission. Again I know people making millions in this way.

Portfolio income

This is investing your money into assets for growth. Some examples of this include:

Stock market: probably the most misunderstood pillar of wealth, the stock market allows you to make money in three market directions: up, down and sideways. The problem is that most people think they can only make money when markets go up and so only make money in one out of three scenarios. This is worse than 50-50 and worse than gambling. So not only can you make money when markets go down (which is amazing), but you can also rent out shares for monthly income when markets go sideways. Most people don't know this but just in the same way as we buy property and then let them out on a monthly basis, called Buy to Let, we can do the buy to let for stocks also, called Buy To Let for Stocks.

For more information on stock market investing and trading (the former is more long term, the latter is more short-term), go to **www.investment-mastery.com**. There is a beginners section and a more advanced section or if you want to go faster, coaching and mentoring also.

Property: one strategy is to buy off-plan before it is built and wait for capital growth. This can only be done in countries where there is substantial growth. The great thing about property is that you only put in 15% - 20 % while the bank lends you more. As the price increases, your money and the money that the bank lends you increases. This means you are making money on OPM – Other People's Money. A great strategy.

Land: Did you know that the land on which the property stands grows in % value faster than the property? Land is the kind of investment that can be good for long term investing – you know what they say, they aren't making any more of it – but you cannot get a mortgage and therefore you only make money on the money you put in, so no OPM.

Which of the above strategies are you doing? The more you do, the better. This is what the Wealth Workout™ is all about ... focusing on multiple streams of income or as we like to call it, as many pillars of wealth as possible holding up your financial freedom structure. Unfortunately, most people just have one pillar, normally their career, holding up the structure. Does this look solid to you? The problem is that if you lose your career, the whole structure comes tumbling down fast, because there are no other pillars holding it in place.

Some people think that having their own business is the answer, but again if this is the only 'pillar' holding up the entire structure then if something happens to the business the whole structure comes tumbling down very fast.

So the more pillars you have holding up the structure, the safer you are and feel. Even if you lost your job, or your business or there is a recession, nothing can hurt you because you have many pillars holding up the structure. It is solid and will hold.

This is what the Wealth Workout™ does – show you how to build up solid pillars of wealth.

Step 5: Compound your returns, by re-investing your profits

The magic of compound returns has been described in many books by many people. Albert Einstein called it the 8th Wonder of the World – well if that is the case, it must be something we need to pay close attention to surely. And yet I am not sure that people really understand it, because otherwise they would be taking action on it. We have already seen the magic of compounding in action when we saw the difference between an 18-year-old saving and a 40-year-old saving. We also saw it with the Financial Freedom Calculator.

But let's take another look at compounding, because it really is that important. Imagine you were a 30-year-old who finds a way of making 12.4% a year on your investments (this is simplicity itself, anyone can do it). You have £1,000 to invest and decide to save £1 a day or £365 a year to add to your investments. If you did that you would have an extra £121,642 at the age of 60. That doesn't rock my boat, what about yours?

Initial amount to invest			£1,000	Enter amount you have to invest	
% Return a Year			12%	Enter the % you wish to achieve a year	
How much can you save a day		£1	£365	Enter the amount of money you can save a day	
Age	30	40	50	60	70
	£1,120	£9,884	£37,103	£121,642	£384,205
	£1,619	£11,435	£41,920	£136,604	£430,675
	£2,179	£13,172	£47,316	£153,361	£482,721
	£2,805	£15,118	£53,359	£172,129	£541,013
	£3,507	£17,297	£60,127	£193,150	£606,299
	£4,293	£19,737	£67,707	£216,693	£679,420
	£5,173	£22,471	£76,197	£243,061	£761,315
	£6,158	£25,533	£85,705	£272,593	£853,038
	£7,262	£28,961	£96,355	£305,669	£955,768
	£8,499	£32,802	£108,283	£342,715	£1,070,825

What could we do to speed up the process? Well, had you started 10 years earlier at 20, that £121,642 would have been worth £384,204 at the age of 60. That's an extra £262,563 in just 10 years.

So what else can you do? Invest more initially? What if we had £2,000 to start with instead of £1,000? With £2,000 to start with and keeping everything else exactly the same, at the age of 60, it would be worth £155,197, which incredibly is a difference of £33,555, considering it was just a £1,000 difference – so the more you start off with the better.

A bit better, but I think we can do even better. What if you were to start with £2,000 – and you could do even more – and instead of saving £1 a day, we save £2 a day, that's £730 a year, what would happen then?

Initial amount to invest			£2,000	Enter amount you have to invest	
% Return a Year			12%	Enter the % you wish to achieve a year	
How much can you save a day		£2	£730	Enter the amount of money you can save a day	
Age	30	40	50	60	70
	£2,240	£19,768	£74,206	£243,283	£768,411
	£3,239	£22,870	£83,841	£273,207	£861,350
	£4,357	£26,344	£94,632	£306,722	£965,442
	£5,610	£30,235	£106,717	£344,259	£1,082,025
	£7,014	£34,594	£120,253	£386,300	£1,212,598
	£8,585	£39,475	£135,414	£433,386	£1,358,840
	£10,345	£44,942	£152,394	£486,122	£1,522,631
	£12,317	£51,065	£171,411	£545,186	£1,706,077
	£14,525	£57,923	£192,710	£611,339	£1,911,536
	£16,998	£65,604	£216,565	£685,429	£2,141,650

Now you have £243,283 in your investment pot. Are you getting the picture? You can do this. But if you were serious about creating wealth, you would do the following:

You would save £5 a day, that's just a measly £150 a month – almost anyone who is willing to give this a go can do this. This calculates to £1,825 a year. But £507,542 at the age of 60 and just under £1 million by the time you retire at 65.

Initial amount to invest			£2,000	Enter amount you have to invest	
% Return a Year			12%	Enter the % you wish to achieve a year	
How much can you save a day		£5	£1,825	Enter the amount of money you can save a day	
Age	30	40	50	60	70
	£2,240	£38,984	£153,103	£507,542	£1,608,376
	£4,334	£45,487	£173,301	£570,272	£1,803,206
	£6,679	£52,770	£195,922	£640,530	£2,021,416
	£9,305	£60,927	£221,258	£719,219	£2,265,811
	£12,247	£70,064	£249,633	£807,350	£2,539,533
	£15,542	£80,296	£281,414	£906,057	£2,846,102
	£19,232	£91,757	£317,009	£1,016,609	£3,189,459
	£23,364	£104,593	£356,875	£1,140,427	£3,574,019
	£27,993	£118,969	£401,525	£1,279,103	£4,004,727
	£33,177	£135,070	£451,533	£1,434,421	£4,487,119

And it gets better. Just look at what happens after that. You could live quite comfortably and still have it growing, couldn't you?

What if you started earlier? What if you had more as an initial investment? What if you saved more than £5 a day? What if you managed to make more than 12% a year?

Personally I would like to see you do this as a minimum: Start off with as close to £5,000 or more, save £10 a day, get 13-15% return or more a year with our help and retire on £2,000,000. That way you can live off the interest and still keep the £2,000,000. Fantastic stuff.

Initial amount to invest			£5,000	Enter amount you have to invest	
% Return a Year			13%	Enter the % you wish to achieve a year	
How much can you save a day		£10	£3,650	Enter the amount of money you can save a day	
Age	30	40	50	60	70
	£5,650	£86,411	£360,561	£1,291,182	£4,450,236
	£10,035	£101,295	£411,084	£1,462,686	£5,032,417
	£14,989	£118,113	£468,175	£1,656,485	£5,690,281
	£20,588	£137,118	£532,688	£1,875,478	£6,433,668
	£26,914	£158,593	£605,588	£2,122,940	£7,273,695
	£34,063	£182,860	£687,964	£2,402,572	£8,222,925
	£42,141	£210,282	£781,049	£2,718,556	£9,295,555
	£51,269	£241,269	£886,236	£3,075,619	£10,507,627
	£61,584	£276,284	£1,005,096	£3,479,099	£11,877,269
	£73,240	£315,851	£1,139,409	£3,935,032	£13,424,964

Some people will have more to invest, some people will have less. Why not tell some friends and family about it and have a fun challenge with them to save and invest more, get more returns etc. and retire financially free unlike everyone else out there.

I challenge you to do it, for yourself and your family.

It is up to you. It always has been and always will be. And you know, the great thing is that this is just your stock market pot – we will teach you how to increase your property portfolio pot, your internet marketing pot etc. at the Wealth Workout™.

What if you had 3-4 pots, each making you £1-2 million?

So you are probably asking yourself *how do you* make 13-15% a year?

We teach you all this at the Wealth Workout™ and much more.

And we show you how to do this tax free. This means that everything you see above will come into your pocket. Directly.

> *Surround yourself only with people who are going to lift you higher.*
>
> *Oprah Winfrey*

6: Create the support team we need

No one expects you to do this all by yourself. In fact, we don't want you to do it by yourself. We think that everyone needs a mentor and/or a coach. What is the difference between the two? Well, a mentor is someone who has already done it, they have made it and they are where you want to be. A good example of this is Sir Richard Branson – would you like to be mentored by this billionaire? Most people would. Unfortunately Sir Richard is busy and therefore unavailable but how about getting a coach?

A coach doesn't need to have done it because they have a toolbox of tools which will get you from where you are now to where you want to go in record time. Let me repeat that – with a coach, you have exponentially increased the chances of getting to where you want to go AND at the same time you have speeded up the process as well. You worry less, sleep better, have more fun and you will get there faster. What a win-win situation.

A lot of people out there would not want to pay for a coach. This is poverty thinking. Would you invest £100 to get back £1,000? Of course you would. So why wouldn't you get a coach to ensure you reach your £2,000,000 mark? Perhaps you think you can do it by yourself? I can tell you that no fortune was ever built alone but required the dedicated help of a team. Napoleon Hill, after spending 25 years studying millionaires and billionaires said that out of 100 things that were important to create riches, these two were the most important:

Having a purpose that is bigger than you (which we have already discussed), and

Forming a Mastermind team.

A mastermind team is made up of people who have the skills and knowledge that you need to get to where you want to go. Here is what a mastermind team is not – a bunch of friends and family getting together with people you like. In fact, you don't even have to like them that much, but you must respect them for the specialised knowledge they have which you want and need in order to create wealth.

This is where the Wealth Workout™ helps. We help you create that Mastermind team of people. We also give you wealth coaching as part of the Wealth Workout™. We also have weekly live calls, physical meetings to do wealth coaching and get trained up by experts.

More about that later.

Education may cost money,
but ignorance is way more expensive.

Claus Moser

7: Take massive consistent wealth actions!

My favourite word in regards to wealth creation has to be 'consistent'. I always say that it does not matter if you only have a few hours a week to dedicate to wealth creation, as long as it is every week. If it is a few hours a month, it has to be every month. The importance of taking action cannot be emphasised enough. I no longer run free live preview seminars - this book replaces that now - but when I did, I used the following metaphor to illustrate a point:

I had a £million note, waved it in the air and asked everyone in the audience, who would like to have it? Everyone assured me that they would. I said, "Who really wants it?" People waved enthusiastically, some people shouted that they would. But no-one moved. So I would say, "Who would do whatever it takes to get this £1million note and suddenly, people realised that they were going to have to do something here, that the money doesn't just drop onto your lap. Inevitably someone near the back would then start to run to the front and someone from the side would rush up, and one person would pip the other to the post and grab the money.

The person who didn't get the money would turn back to their seat a little dejected but I would say, "Hold on, where are you going? I thought you wanted £1 million?" They would blink at me, not fully understanding, so I explained, "What makes you think that there is just one £1 million? There is enough for everyone who is willing to take action" and then I would give them a £1 million as well.

I would then turn to the audience and say, "What was the difference between what they just did and everyone else?" And they would shout, "They took action!" I would reply, "That's right. In life, people sit there, saying they want money and it is right there for them to take but they don't do anything about it ... so how important is taking action?" Everyone would shout that it is extremely important. So I would say, "Are you sure you understand how important it is? Let's find out ..." and I would wave another £1 million note.

Now everyone would get up and we would have a lot of fun with it.

I guess what I am doing now is waving this £1 million note at you and asking, "Who wants it? Do you want it?" And you can shout and wave but unless you take any action on this, the £1 million will never appear in your bank account.

<u>It is now up to you to take action</u>. **Are you ready ?!**

How the Wealth Workout™ can make your dreams come true

The Wealth Workout™ is a proven wealth and success system

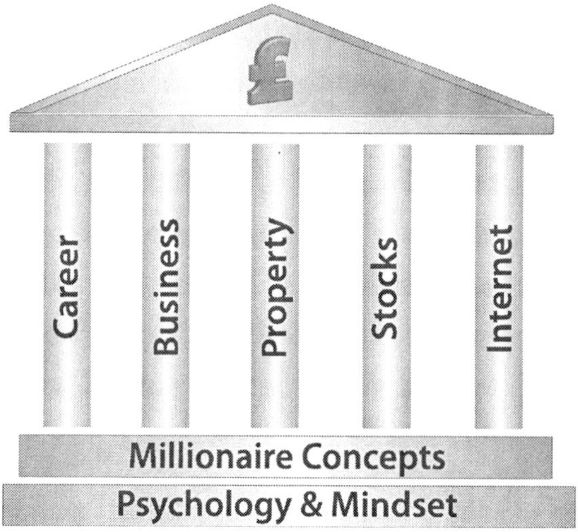

It builds you a solid foundation of wealth mindset so that nothing can stop you from creating wealth on which to build your millionaire concepts and then the 5 pillars of wealth.

First and foremost, it will help you face the facts of where you stand financially, whether you are in debt, whether you are barely breaking even or doing well, and calculates your net worth, the only true measure of your wealth.

It asks the question – do you want to be in the top 1% of the population that reach financial freedom, or the next 5% who are financially independent and no longer have to work?

In terms of mindset and psychology, the absolute foundation of any wealth creation strategy, the Wealth Workout™ gives you the tools to be in the top 1% of the population. You will eliminate the beliefs that are keeping you poor and replace them with the psychology of the rich and attract wealth. You will understand and be able to apply financial concepts of rich - what the rich invest in which the poor and middle class do not and how to get into the good habits of the wealthy.

We give you the financial freedom planner because poor people don't plan – the rich plan. That's a fact. You will learn other millionaire concepts to ensure that you build a solid financial structure.

On top of this you will build the 5 pillars, which are taught by our rotating Wealth Faculty. These are people who have not only made it, they are willing to share it with you. If you were to put the faculty in one room, they would account for £60 million worth of assets.

I will briefly explain what they cover below:

Property in UK – either let the experts build up a £million property portfolio for you or they can teach you how to do it do – whichever you prefer (I prefer both!).

International Properties – Another expert will explain why the UK may not be the best place to invest and why you should consider focusing on other countries for growth. Again, I like to do it all.

Business – one of our faculty is called the Millionaire's Coach because he has taken 14 different people who were at different stages in their business and made their businesses so profitable that they became millionaires. Wouldn't you want to be coached by this person? I did, so I hired him and he is now my business coach.

Business millionaire – These guys are very busy so they rotate but one of them made a £ million in just three days work ... on two separate occasions. If he can do it in a few days, surely you can do it in a lifetime? Another Business millionaire recently sold his business for £10million and goes through the story of how he started from a broken down council flat, married with 6 children ... and you think you've got it tough?

Stock market – one of the most misunderstood of the 5 pillars, the stock market makes millionaires automatically ... if you start early. I will personally be revealing a step-by-step strategy where you make an average of 15% a year in just 2 hours a year. So simple your children can do it ... and it's fun.

Internet Marketing – the baby of the pillars of wealth. But boy is it exciting. We have a rotating faculty who have 30-100 websites each. One of our faculty turns over £1 million a year from his living room. You are going to want to know how he does this and carve out your fair share.

Your follow up support

We believe that the learning starts at the end of the course so we follow up with you for as long as it takes:

- Weekly conference calls
- Physical meetings every other month
- Coaching sessions
- Wealth consultations
- Members-only Website and Wealth Club with online forum support

Your 100% money back guarantee

If after one year of using the workbook, conference calls and attending the meetings you believe you can't make ten times your money back, then simply and discreetly let us know and we will refund you 100% Guaranteed.

I hope this sounds good but we have a wide range of financial education materials for you so we need to ascertain whether this is right for you or not.

The reason that most people don't take any action is because they are scared. It is not always certain what they are fearful of, but it is often of the unknown. Is this going to cost me money? Investing in your education does cost money, I should know, I have spent over £60,000 on my financial education, but it pays off again and again and again. Once you have the information you can use it for the rest of your life. You can teach your family, children and friends. Put it this way, you might think that education costs money, but you should try ignorance, it is a lot more expensive. Invest in yourself first and foremost.

Marcus, where do I start?

Take advantage of our FREE Offer now call 0870 835 2260 for your FREE Financial Freedom Breakthrough Session worth £197... absolutely FREE with this book.

One of our friendly team will take you through the financial freedom consultation so you can see where you are now and where you need to go, and the things you can do to speed up that process.

They will also take you through your own personal compounding sheet which is not affected by taxes.

The cost of not taking action.

I will leave you with a last thought. If you carry on doing what you are doing currently, then what result are you going to get?

Is it possible that doing the same things will get you the same results as now?

But now imagine that you did something different and received a financial education, then what could happen?

Call one of our team now and let them know what you thought about the book and enquire about our **FREE Financial Freedom Breakthrough sessions**.

Don't wait another second –

Call 0870 835 2260 NOW!

Remember that we are here to help, so simply contact us and I look forward to speaking with you very soon.

To your Wealth!

Marcus de Maria

Wealth Workout - Wealth Creation course

"I came to the workshop as a cynic and left feeling converted. It has opened my eyes on my future and the need to invest and plan and to have confidence in myself" **Alan O.**

"If you want to add some great tools to your money making toolbox, this workout is fantastic value!!!!" **Jason E.**

"Marcus and his team have put together a superb weekend to help people make great investment choices that sets them up for life. The opportunity to speak with the speakers who generously gave their advice was invaluable and exceeded my expectations." **Kate D.**

"Its incredible! A good platform to succeed with like minded-individuals. It's a must! A+++++" **Ambar H.**

"If I had the money, I would pay people to attend this workshop - it has really changed my life and the way I look at life. I am a changed person" **Michael T.**

"This is the most unique workshop creating wealth around. It's like a one stop shop for all the different investment vehicles for creating wealth...all in one" **Abdi M.**

"Absolutely brilliant. I owe you so much Marcus. The educational, non-biased method of being taught financial concepts is outstanding and everyone should be here." **Martyn R.**

"Extremely useful and complete information, very well presented, entertaining, inspiring. I could not have spent my weekend any better." **Petra L.**

"I came to get a clearer picture of what I would like to achieve. It exceeded my expectations." **Tom B.**

"Excellent value for money. I've learnt such a lot, especially about investing in property and Internet marketing which was completely new to me. Many thanks for the great wealth workout. I'm inspired to get my financial act together." **Mary P.**

"An incredible introduction to the psychology for wealth, backed by real, tangible, practical methods of achieving wealth and success! A fantastic overview of the five pillars of wealth and how to apply them in the real world." **Phil S.**

"If you are feeling stuck, struggling with the financial area of your life or already successful and wanting to step up to the next level, I can highly recommend the Wealth Workout. It's the ultimate buffet of Wealth creation delights" **Tom M.**

"The shares were excellent! A huge amount of information, need time to assimilate it! Great to hear this information in an inspirational and supportive environment. Giving us homeplay and follow up support excellent idea. " **Catherine E.**

"It was a good basis to understand which necessary steps I had to do. I learned a lot and it was a great benefit for me. I can and will recommend this course to other people as well." **Birgit W.**

"This is of massive benefit. I feel I have learned how to increase the wealth of my existing business as well as creating simple income streams that are time efficient and achievable. It was a fun entertaining and action packed weekend. Thank you." **Hazel M.**

"If you want to get a good overview on investments and possible vehicles to suit you, then this is perfect. Marcus gives great value for money. There is no hype or wild promises. The subject were treated thoroughly and sensibly with various options to consider." **Alan J.**

"A course where you have your horizons expanded and your mind opened to ideas of wealth and success. You find out that we can all do it. It completely exceeded my expectation." **Lance D.**

"Fantastic. Such a brilliant realisation that I have so many options at my fingertips and that I must now start to achieve my vision. So many new ideas! Great mix of presentations." **Mel C.**

Investment Mastery
Your road map to financial freedom™
Call 0870 835 2260 / 61 www.investment-mastery.com
Did you know at just 3% returns per month (36% per year) you could be financially free in 6 years. Free of debt; free of worrying about money. Free to choose if you work or not. Free to spend your time as you want.
Marcus de Maria
AS FEATURED IN SHARES MAGAZINE
AS FEATURED IN MONEYWISE MAGAZINE
AS FEATURED IN INSIDE BUSINESS MAGAZINE
AS FEATURED IN SUNDAY BUSINESS NEWSPAPER
Absolute experts in teaching you to create wealth in the stock market
Workshops and 1-1 mentoring

Investment Mastery - Stock Market workshop

"The content was perfect. I liked the way Marcus gave everyone the opportunity to ask questions and he gave straight answers. Marcus is prepared to share knowledge acquired through years of experience. INVALUABLE. I liked the options especially!" **Claudia G.**

"Far exceeded my expectations. Presentation was well paced, and allowed people at all levels to have their questions answered." **Anthony W.**

"This is the place to start if you want to invest in the stock market but aren't sure what to do. 3 strategies are taught and practiced. Lots of time to ask questions and get your answers." **Jacquie T.**

"Marcus' workshop makes it easier than mere seminars because you are actually trading. You practice a few times in the workshop and it clicks. I know I'll be trading next week because it's so simple. If I don't then there is always the follow up support" **Lionel J.**

"This is a good workshop that covers a lot of ground, presented with a light hearted humour. Obviously the use of a computer each to practice on and the support was much appreciated." **Sunil T.**

"It exploded the myth about stock market. Liked the short term strategy. My buddy was very supportive and overall felt that the course was a good investment" **Jo V.**

"The organisation and content of the Workshop were at high level. The course opened new horizons for me and showed me new opportunities to achieve our goals. I really liked small group exercises, using computers and practising during the course itself. " **Chris N.**

"I feel I have a much better understanding of stocks and options now. The workshop is fast paced but there are plenty of opportunities to ask questions. It was presented clearly and with humour. It was made clear that there will be a lot of opportunities to clarify things we may not have "got" through the weekly phone calls and meetings" **Jane H.**

"There was an enormous amount of knowledge shared within the 2 days. I believe it is something that every beginner needs to attend" **Natasha O.**

"I very much liked the hands on approach using the computers; this was streets ahead of what I experienced elsewhere." **Walid A.**

"It was a good size class and we felt comfortable asking questions. Good explanations were given to all questions. We

gained clarity and confidence on how to place a trade and get started in baby steps with view to moving to more complex trades in the future. It's a great start and am excited to get started, finally! Also I like the fact that we have the opportunity to share ideas in the monthly meetings and conference calls."
Heide G.

"Fantastic workshop! Very practical - I loved that we were a small group doing virtual trading - I can now go home and practise. Great to be encouraged to buddy up and exchange contact details. Love the ongoing support. Marcus has a very engaging, motivating, honest manner - great to listen to."
Rani D.

"I recommend that serious future traders start with Investment Mastery." **Colin O.**

"An extremely helpful first step guide to investing online - be prepared to work hard and follow up afterwards. No other workshop provides the same level of one to one attention or chance to try things." **Kush C.**

"This is a hands on workshop. It gets you up and running from the very beginning and successfully mixes enough theory with practical doing." **Paul C.**

Printed in the United Kingdom by
Lightning Source UK Ltd., Milton Keynes
137308UK00002BA/136-840/P